AF480921

US AND BRITISH MILITARY LEADERS DURING THE AMERICAN REVOLUTION

History of the United States

Children's History Books

Speedy Publishing LLC
40 E. Main St. #1156
Newark, DE 19711
www.speedypublishing.com

In this book, we're going to talk about Military Leaders during the American Revolution. So, let's get right to it!

FLAG OF UNITED STATES OF AMERICA

The thirteen colonies in America fought the British to win their independence. From 1765 to 1783, the battles were fought on American soil with strong military leaders on both sides of the conflict.

The British were well known as a world power but the Americans didn't have a strong military force to begin with. However, the Americans had much to gain and more to lose by not winning the battle to create an independent country of their own. The British and the French had long been enemies, so some French military men fought with the colonists against the British.

CONTINENTAL ARMY MILITARY LEADERS

GEORGE WASHINGTON

George Washington

In May 1775, the Continental Congress selected George Washington to be the commander general of the army. The British army was well trained and Washington had a difficult task. His "soldiers" were mainly farmers and had not been trained specifically for fighting.

However, Washington was a great leader and over the six years of active fighting he kept marching forward and leading the army of the new nation on to victory. One of his famous battles was the Crossing of the Delaware on Christmas Day in 1776. Washington led his troops on a surprise attack and captured 1,000 Hessian soldiers. The Hessians were from Germany and had been hired by the British to fight in the war.

NATHANAEL GREENE

NATHANAEL GREENE

When the war began, Green was a low ranking soldier—a militia private. However, as he fought under the leadership of Washington, he gained a stellar reputation as a very talented officer. Washington placed him in command of the Southern Campaign. In the Carolinas, he and his soldiers fought off General Cornwallis.

They were successful and Cornwallis and his forces were driven out and went to Virginia. Greene was a Quaker and the Quakers were committed to peace so he struggled with that internal battle while he was in the military. Despite this, he decided to fight for the cause of America's freedom.

A PEACEABLE KINGDOM WITH QUAKERS BEARING BANNERS

HENRY KNOX

Henry Knox

As a young man, Knox owned a bookstore in Boston that catered to British officers and became a popular spot for Boston aristocrats. He had lots of books on military science, which was one of his many interests. After the city began to boycott goods that were coming from Britain, his profits decreased. He married into a family of British Loyalists.

When the war erupted, Henry and his wife fled from Boston, leaving their business to be looted, and he joined the Patriots in their fight against the British. Knox eventually became George Washington's chief artillery officer. At the end of the war, Knox became the first Secretary of War.

HENRY KNOX

JEAN BAPTISTE DE ROCHAMBEAU

Jean Baptiste de Rochambeau

Rochambeau was a French general and nobleman. He was commander-in-chief of the French troops who traveled from Europe to help the colonists defeat the British in the Revolutionary War

In 1781, his 7,000 French troops departed from Rhode Island and joined Washington's forces on the Hudson River in New York. In September of that same year, these combined forces gathered with the troops of the Marquis de Lafayette and they were able to get Cornwallis and his British army to surrender at Yorktown in Virginia.

JEAN BAPTISTE DE ROCHAMBEAU

FRANCOIS JOSEPH PAUL DE GRASSE

Francois Joseph Paul de Grasse

A French admiral, Grasse led troops to victory at the Battle of the Capes. This victory halted the British ships from their mission to reinforce the troops at Yorktown, Virginia. Since the British forces weren't strengthened, this action indirectly helped ensure that Cornwallis would surrender at Yorktown, which ultimately led to the end of the war.

Horatio Gates

Gates was a British soldier who had retired from the Royal Army. He became a very controversial general of the Revolutionary war. He, along with others, tried to get George Washington replaced during the scandal of the Conway Cabal.

HORATIO GATES

CONTINENTAL CONGRESS, JUNE 15TH 1775

This scandal began when a French-Irish brigadier general by the name of Thomas Conway sent scathing letters to the Second Continent Congress. The letters criticized Washington. When the content of the text was brought to the public's attention, Washington's supporters rallied around him.

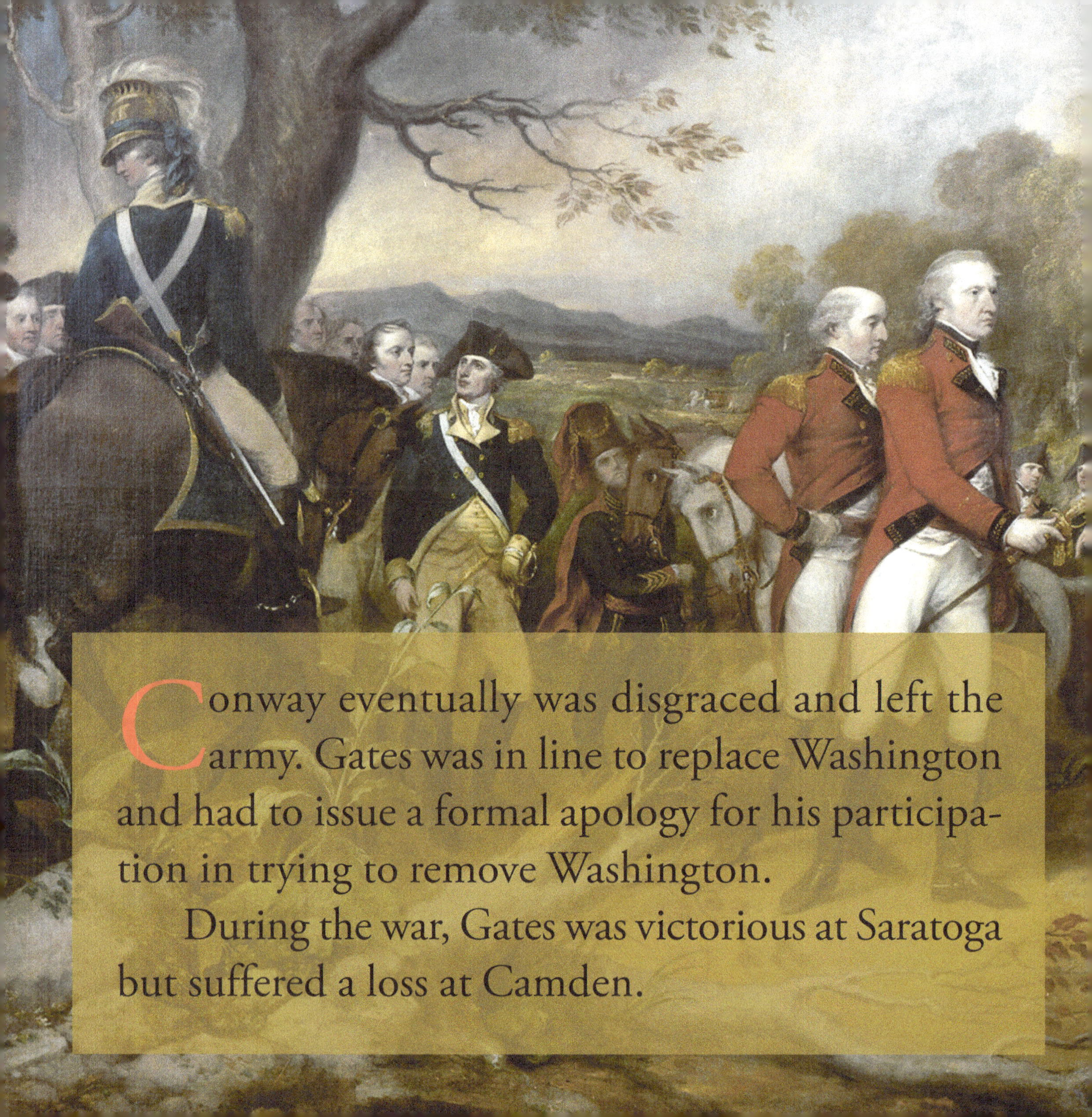

Conway eventually was disgraced and left the army. Gates was in line to replace Washington and had to issue a formal apology for his participation in trying to remove Washington.

During the war, Gates was victorious at Saratoga but suffered a loss at Camden.

SURRENDER OF GENERAL BURGOYNE AT SARATOGA, NEW YORK.

DANIEL MORGAN

Daniel Morgan

In 1775, Congress decided that 10 rifle companies should be formed for reinforcements for the Siege of Boston, which lasted over ten months. The Virginia assembly chose Daniel Morgan to lead one of the rifle companies.

He quickly recruited about 100 men in a little over a week and then organized them before they set out for a 600-mile march to Boston. His marksmen, aimed with lightweight rifles, marched into Boston in 21 days.

His militia group was called "Morgan's Riflemen." His rifleman used what are today called guerilla strategies to attack the British. The British fought in very formal ways and they considered this type of fighting to be dishonorable.

MORGAN'S RIFLEMEN

MARQUIS DE LAFAYETTE

Marquis de Lafayette

De Lafayette was a wealthy French aristocrat who played an important part both in the Revolutionary War as well as the French Revolution. He was appointed as a major general before France had agreed to fight for the colonists and reported to George Washington during most of the war. He is famous for helping to lead the American troops against the British troops at the siege of Yorktown. He was one of Washington's trusted friends and warned him about the Conway Cabal.

John Paul Jones

John Paul Jones is famous for his bravery in America's Navy. He felt that Scotland had been not treated well by the British, so he was for the American colonies. He came to America to fight and he came at a good time because, despite his checkered past, the Continental Navy needed captains and enlisted him right away.

JOHN PAUL JONES

Between voyages, he met and became friends with Benjamin Franklin. He is best known for defeating the Serapis while commanding his ship, the Bonhomme Richard, which was named after Benjamin Franklin's "Poor Richard's Almanac." When the captain for the Serapis asked Jones to surrender he spoke the now-famous line "I have not yet begun to fight!".

BRITISH MILITARY LEADERS

WILLIAM HOWE

William Howe

Howe was commander-in-chief of the British troops from the years 1776 to 1778. Earlier, while in Parliament, he had sided with the American colonies against the British Intolerable Acts. However, after the Battle at Bunker Hill, he no longer aligned himself with the colonies.

At the beginning of the war, he was winning and losing battles at an even pace. But, during the battle of Princeton when he didn't capture Washington and lost his opportunity not once but twice, his career started to go downhill.

Henry Clinton

Henry Clinton fought alongside Howe, Burgoyne, and Gage during the siege of Boston at the start of the war. His clear-headed decisions helped them to break the siege. Later that same year, after General William Howe replaced Thomas Gage as the British troops' commander, Henry Clinton was appointed second in command.

HENRY CLINTON

CHARLES CORNWALLIS

Charles Cornwallis

General Charles Cornwallis successfully led troops to victory in many battles during the American Revolution including the Battle of Long Island in 1776 and also the Battle of Brandywine in 1777.

He was given command of the British army fighting the battles in the southern part of the colonies in 1779. At first, he was victorious but then after running out of troops as well as resources, he was forced to concede defeat at Yorktown, Virginia, which signaled the end of the war.

John Burgoyne

General John Burgoyne came up with a plan of attack. He planned to travel with his troops south from Canada and divide up New England. He and his troops were moving slowly and this allowed the Americans to regroup.

JOHN BURGOYNE

When he got to New York instead of finding other British troops to help him with his plan, he found that the army had relocated to fight and capture Philadelphia. He fought near

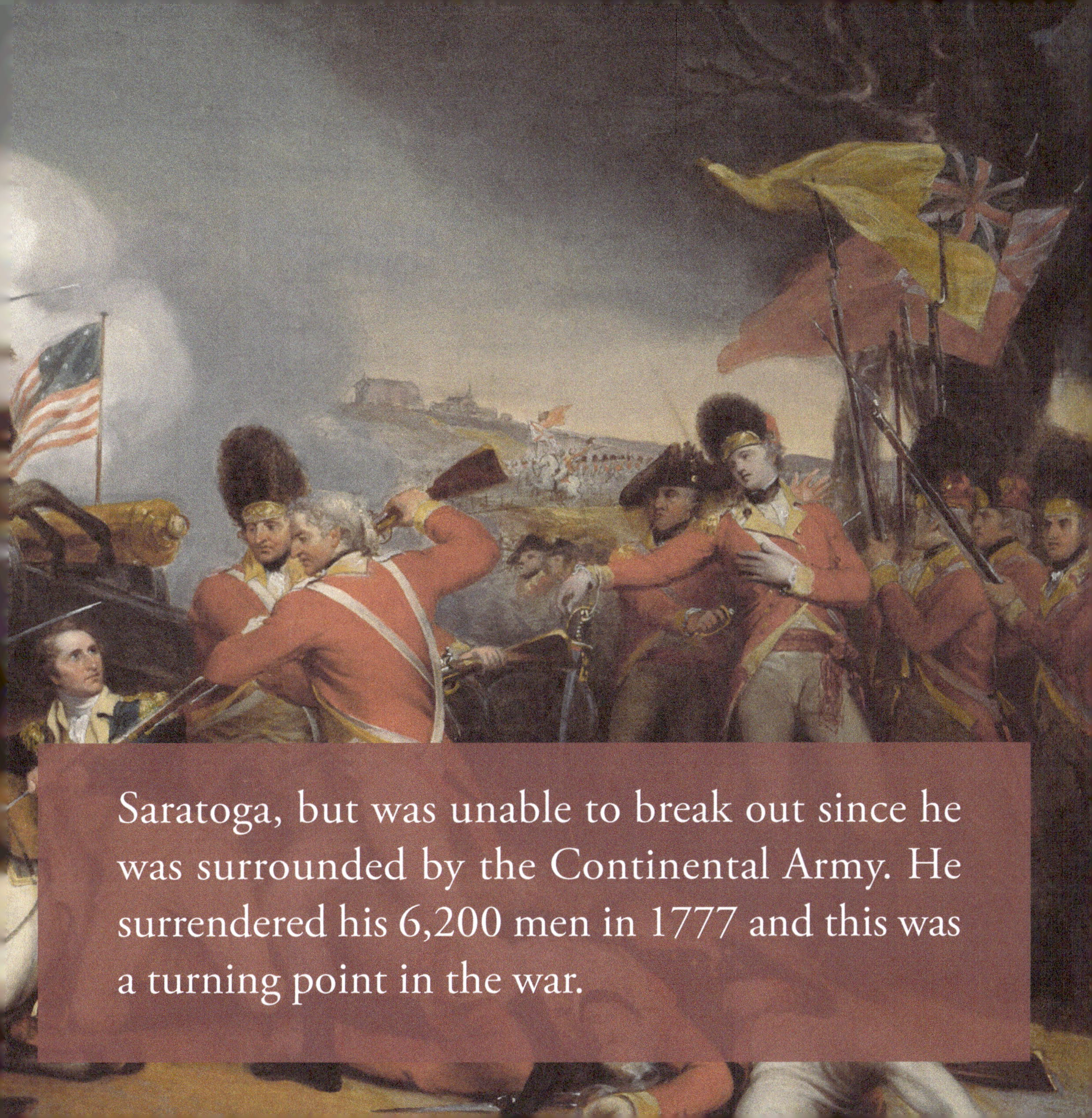

Saratoga, but was unable to break out since he was surrounded by the Continental Army. He surrendered his 6,200 men in 1777 and this was a turning point in the war.

Thomas Gage

Thomas Gage was the commander-in-chief of the British army during the early part of the war. Ironically, eight years before that appointment he had fought alongside George Washington in the French and Indian War.

THOMAS GAGE

A FAMOUS TRAITOR

Benedict Arnold

Even today if you call someone a "Benedict Arnold," it means that that person is a traitor and has gone over to the other side. Arnold led Continental troops at Fort Ticonderoga as well as in the Battle of Saratoga. He then decided to switch sides and began fighting as a brigadier general for the British.

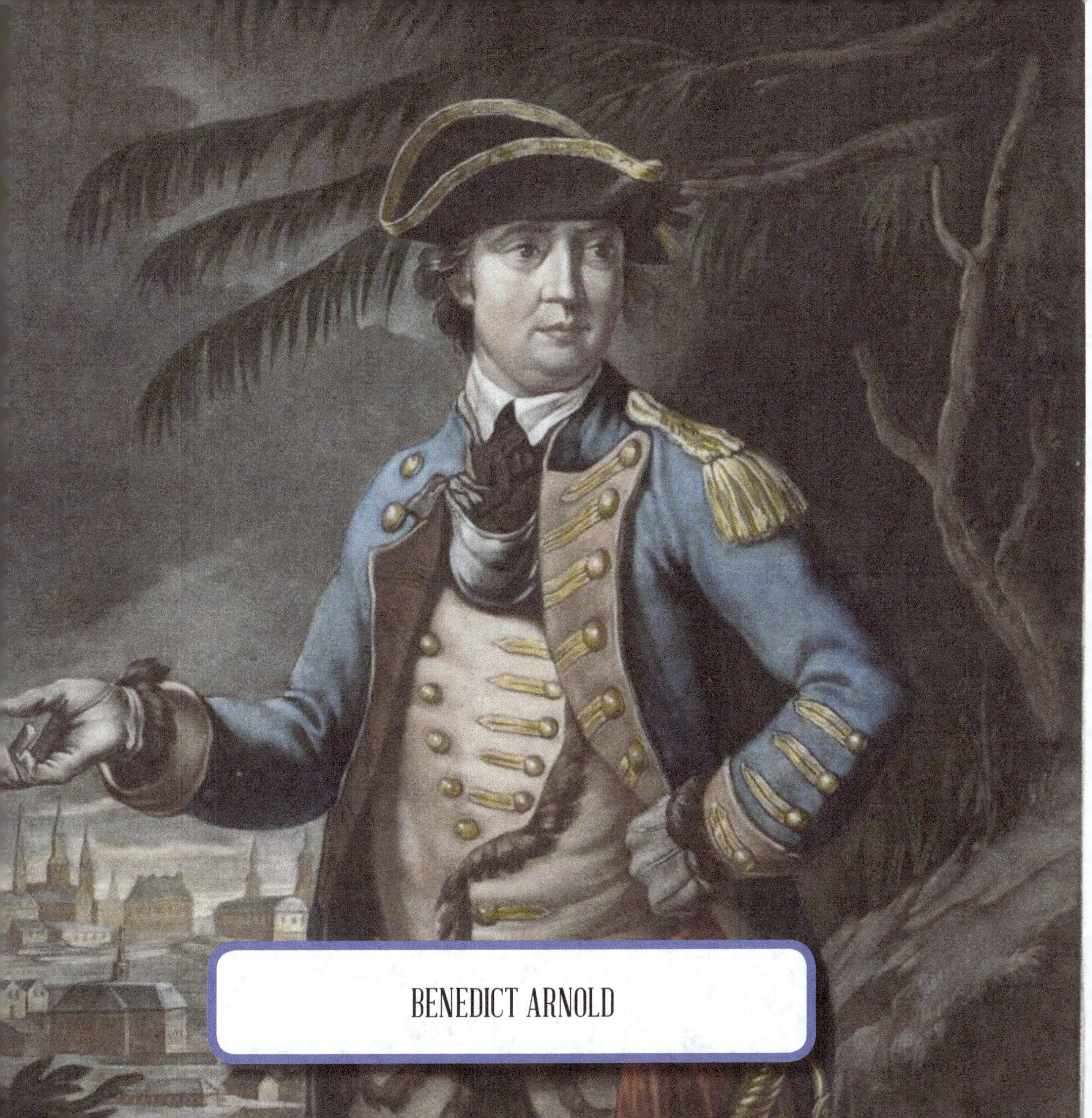
BENEDICT ARNOLD

Awesome! Now you know more about the great Military Leaders on both sides of the American Revolution. You can find more History books from Baby Professor by searching the website of your favorite book retailer.

Visit

BABY PROFESSOR
EDUCATION KIDS

www.BabyProfessorBooks.com

to download Free Baby Professor eBooks and view our catalog of new and exciting Children's Books

www.ingramcontent.com/pod-product-compliance
Lightning Source LLC
Chambersburg PA
CBHW081603120726
47973CB00045B/73

* 9 7 9 8 8 6 9 4 1 0 4 4 3 *